BETTER THAN EVER: A 30 Day Reflective Devotional

ISBN: 978-0-578-54852-4

LOC: 2019910260

Copyright: LaRissa Oxner and Sherry Smalls

Publisher: Fiery Beacon Consulting and Publishing Group

Graphic Artist: Tiffany Jeffers, HIS Design Services

This work was produced in Greensboro, North Carolina, United States of America.

All rights reserved under International Copyright Law.

Unless otherwise noted, all scripture references have been presented from the New King James version or Common English version of the bible. All definitions have been presented by *Dictionary.com*. Contents and/or cover may not be reproduced in whole or in part in any form without the expressed written consent of the Authors LaRissa Oxner and Sherry Smalls.

BETTER THAN EVER:

A 30-Day Self-Reflective Devotional

By LaRissa Oxner and Sherry Smalls

TABLE OF CONTENTS

The Dedication

A Message from Sherry

A Message from LaRissa

Day 1: The Breakdown for the Build Up 15
Day 2: Don't Pick Your Scabs 18
Day 3: Journey to Joy 21
Day 4: Validation 23
Day 5: Confidence 26
Day 6: You are Enough 28
Day 7: The Present is a Gift 32
Day 8: Don't Compare…Conquer! 35
Day 9: Don't Get Ready - Stay Ready 38
Day 10: The Time Has Come 41
Day 11: Commit to the Process 44
Day 12: Pint-Size Wisdom: Dare to be Different 48
Day 13: The Outward Look to Reflect an Inward Change... 51
Day 14: It's Okay 54
Day 15: Be Disruptive 57
Day 16: Don't Drop the Glass Balls 60
Day 17: Setting Boundaries (Part 1) 62

Day 18: Set the Boundaries Then Clean Your Clutter (Part 2)...... 64

Day 19: God did not Give them the Vision, so do not Expect Them to Understand Your Dreams 67

Day 20: Create the Community You Deserve 70

Day 21: You are the Superpower 73

Day 22: Reset! Recharge! Rest! 76

Day 23: Foundation Matters 79

Day 24: Perception is Reality 82

Day 25: Access Granted 86

Day 26: Do the Work 89

Day 27: Go On and Be Great 92

Day 28: Play to Win 95

Day 29: Celebrate Always 98

Day 30: Better Than Ever 100

Connect With Us

Sherry's Dedication

To my Mommie: I thank you for your strength and resiliency; no matter what challenges life brings, you handle it with grace and unrelenting faith. Thank you for providing me with love and a strong spiritual foundation. You have always been my #1 Fan, prayer warrior, and supporter. You were the first person to believe in me and I love you more than words can say. It's your time now!

To my Husband -My college sweetheart, my protector: You have supported me, challenged me, prayed for me, grown with me, and loved me unconditionally. Thank you for being my co-pilot on this journey of life, we are just getting started. Love you babe.

Lastly to the three most amazing gifts God could have ever given me Aaron, Ethan, and Isaac: I pray you always know that you are all destined for greatness and even now begin to live in your own purpose. You three have pushed and inspired me more than you will ever know. May this book serve as an example, that if you dream it, the reality of it can manifest. I hope to make you as proud of me as I am of you. I love you with my whole heart.

LaRissa's Dedication

I dedicate this Devotional to every person that has ever felt broken. I serve a living testimony that you can overcome anything and be fully restored.

Family is everything to me.

To my family: Through blood and spirit, we stand together always, support one another, and pray for one another. I love you all with an unconditional love.

To my Mommy, the Queen in my life: Where would I be without you? You are so strong, loving, caring - I could go on and on. Thank you for loving me. Thank you for providing and protecting me. Thank you for always being there for me without judgement, but always holding me accountable. I love you with every part of me Mommy. I know that you are proud of me, but I am even more proud to be your daughter. I have watched you war through life and come out victorious every time. Thank you for teaching me to be the best mom I can be. Thank you for showing me that giving up is never an option. I only pray that God gives me the same strength, grace and wisdom given to you as I raise my daughter.

To my baby Mia: You are my whole world. I am better because of you. I love you so much and I dedicate this devotional to you. You are valuable. You are worthy. You are loved and supported. Never accept anything less than God's best for you. You are my muse. You are the reason I get up in the morning and handle life. You drive me to be the best person I can be. You are full of joy and light. Shine on. May these writings keep you humble, wise, and strong. May these words bring you comfort, peace, and joy when times get hard. Remember, you are a world changer. You are unstoppable. Get it Boop Boop!

A Message from Sherry

As you scroll through these pages my hope is that you find this collection to be one of inspiration and encouragement. The truth is we all wear so many hats but sometimes we need to take all those hats, sit them down, look in the mirror, bare of all titles and responsibilities and affirm that WE ARE ALL ENOUGH. God has truly formed you beautifully and made you wonderfully. There is not one thing you can do to add to your worth in God and nothing you can do that would take it away.

We often get so bogged down with everyone else's needs and expectations of us that we neglect or never discover the very essence of who we are. I hope this book serves as a pick me up for whatever roller coaster life takes you on with the assurance that you are not alone in this journey. It is through these trials that we become triumphant. There is a silent and underutilized sisterhood of women, mothers, daughters, friends that all deal with issues from life changes, abuse, neglect, depression, worthiness, love, trust, temptation, and fear (just to name a few). How great would it be to lean on that sisterhood knowing that we all struggle in various ways and yet all want the very best that life can offer? God has birthed so many gifts and talents in each of us that lay dormant waiting for us to recognize those talents and reach our full potential. The amazing thing about the gifts that God gives is that we were born with all the essential tools needed to live in our purpose. Please consider this my personal invitation to use these moments to self-reflect and consider- are you living in your purpose and are you pursing your life's passion? There is never a better time than now to Reinvent your Destiny.

Self-check: Superwoman is a fictitious character!

A Message from LaRissa

      I am so glad you have made the choice that no matter what challenges come, you will walk in the truth -you are more than a conqueror! There are so many highs and lows in our lives that have us questioning purpose and how it all fits; I assure you there is a great purpose and a tailor-made plan to give you abundant life. Your identity may have gotten lost in the rubble of trials and tribulations, but it will be found. Your heart may be hurting due to all the disappoints that are too many to count, but it will be mended. Everything you thought you lost is being returned to you even now. You will smile again. You will have joy. I encourage you not to quit in the middle of your journey but to embrace the process toward your promise and future. Gain strength, inspiration, and empowerment from the stories shared in this safe place. Allow this 30-Day Self-Reflective Devotional to remind you of the beauty that lies in every part of your existence. You have come too far to quit! The best is yet to come.

Self-check: You Got This.

Day 1

The Break Down for a Build Up!

Imagine planning a life with someone you love only to receive a phone call from a woman claiming to be your lover's wife. I was totally devastated, hurt and confused as one could imagine. There I was leaving a meeting full of promise with joy in my heart excited to share the great news with my love and with one phone call the world I knew was destroyed. What just happened? Is this true? How could I have missed this? These were just some of the questions that quickly clouded my mind. I was hurt and angry at the betrayal and there was no doubt I wanted that man to suffer as I was suffering, but I chose to take the negative and turn it into a positive. See, I was already on the road of creating a bountiful life; full of joy, wealth, and peace. This was a sure sign that the person I was connected to was not part of the plan.

Love and companionship are things we all long for, but we have to be mindful of the connections we make. So many times, we allow ourselves to be seduced by temporary pleasures while searching for lasting effects - this will not work. Everyone is not capable of carrying the mantle of being your partner nor will everyone be able to participate in your future.

Trust and love yourself enough to know that you are valuable and very capable of handling anything that comes your way. There will be times you will have to travel roads alone; it is all part of the build-up. If you have suffered any type of hurt and pain at the hands of another, I encourage you to take strength from me, gather the pieces of your brokenness and turn it into a masterpiece of victory; I made it through this and you can too. One of my favorite scriptures in the bible is Jeremiah 29:11:

"For I know the plans I have for you," declares the Lord, "plans to prosper you and not to harm you, plans to give you hope and a future."

My breakdown only built me up. Leaving the past behind, I began to clearly focus on loving myself. I surrounded myself with great support. I made the decision to continue my journey toward a hopeful and prosperous future, I chose to stop at nothing to become *Better Than Ever.*

Self-Check:

Everybody can't go.

Day 2

Don't Pick Your Scabs

One of the magical things about the body is its ability to heal itself but healing is more than something that takes place in the body due to sickness or trauma; it is also a process that must take place in the mind.

I loved growing up at my Granny's farmhouse. My male cousins and I would play outside most of the day and between the stick bushes and the dirt ditches I was bound to get hurt. For fear that my granny would make me stop playing and go inside I would cover up and hide my wounds. When the wounds started to heal, I developed a habit of picking the scabs. Once I removed the hard, dark, and unattractive covering the wound would start to bleed again. I did not care about the bleeding and no one could tell I was hurt unless they walked up on me; I just did not want the scabs to show. One day my mother asked why I kept picking my scabs - I remember telling her it was because the scabs were hard, dark, and ugly and I did not want anyone to see it. She said, "if you do not stop picking the scabs your wounds will not be protected while your body does its job to heal." A scab's purpose by definition is to provide protection over a cut or wound as it heals.

My mother taught me a great lesson that day: what I considered to be ugly, hard, and unattractive was the very thing that was necessary for my healing; I had never thought about that. We all have things that we want to hide for fear that it will expose vulnerable places in our lives like those dark, ugly, and unattractive heart breaks, broken dreams, or failed attempts at success. We would like to forget them and just go on with our lives, but things we try to hide always have a way of showing up just like the blood that kept reminding me that my wound was not healed. May I suggest that sometimes hiding these moments inside ourselves does more harm than good? Not sharing your truths could be holding you back from your healing or the healing of others. My mother freed me that day and today I would like to free you. Maybe you have fallen or been hurt and bruised - do not hide by picking your scabs. Know that you are fully protected and covered and that you have the power to heal.

Self-Check

What are you holding on to that is keeping you from your healing?

"**If you don't face it, you will not be able to fix it."** (Stephen Lawrence)

_____
_____
_____
_____
_____
_____
_____
_____
_____
_____
_____
_____
_____
_____
_____
_____
_____

Day 3

Journey to Joy

Sometimes the most hurtful words can be exactly what you need to hear for clarity. This was never more true than when the man I adored told me that *my* happiness was not his job, that *my* happiness was a choice. After crying my heart out from the feeling of losing my prince charming I was able to accept the truth in his words. I had to acknowledge that I had put the pressure of my wants and happiness on to someone else as I took a non-active role, and audaciously had high expectation to have this elated feeling all the time. I relinquished my power to him to dictate and control the environment. It was easier to give him that task instead of sitting with myself, trying to figure out, learn and discover what it was that I needed for myself to receive an internal long-lasting feeling which I could identify as joy and not happiness.

Not only did I have to take ownership of this, but I had to be responsible for it and be willing to do the work to make the changes needed. I do not believe that as women, many of us were taught how to give ourselves self-care, or how to self-love but instead we were taught to protect our hearts, and never let anyone see our frailties. I believe if we were taught that self-love and care was not selfish, we would be less tolerant to things we allow or accept in our lives. When I began to consider things I allowed to enter my life that did not bring me joy, I realized I had a lot of work to do; more than that, I needed to understand why I allowed those things to enter my life and be willing to do something about it.

Self-Check:

Your happiness is up to you.

Day 4

Validation

"It's not that we think we are qualified to do anything on our own, our qualification comes from God." (2 Cor.3:5.) The word validation is defined as:

"**the action of checking or providing validity or accuracy of something; found to be acceptable which is to be received as adequate or suitable.**"

I often struggle with this word as it relates to my successes and accomplishments - to strive for excellence all for the sake of people finding me "adequate or suitable". I would like to point the blame of this internal feeling of not being enough on some strange childhood mishap, the color of my skin, or my gender and perhaps there is a role each one of those things play in my feelings of inadequacy, but if I am honest I think it is a combination of it all mixed with the reality that I do not know where this feeling originated. My desire to feel suitable often becomes unsurmountable when crippled with fear, because the opposite of validation for me is rejection. I find myself retreating from sharing my ideas and dreams for fear of disapproval and wrestling with the knowledge that no one's approval should be needed. Yet I still yearn to be acknowledged by those closest to me, when the truth is my greatness did not come from those I seek the approval of. I struggle to constantly remind myself that my greatness comes from God and that alone not only validates me but warrants me worthy of all that He has blessed me with.

Consciously I decide that no man or woman's approval can override what God has in store for me. People's opinions, whether favorable or unfavorable, do not qualify me and will not propel me toward my goals; neither you nor I need permission to pursue our passion(s) - we just have to be present and persistent. I have learned to not only encourage myself but to celebrate my wins both big and small in ways that matter to me.

Self-Check:

You are as great as God intended for you to be, you just have to believe and accept it.

_____
_____
_____
_____
_____
_____
_____
_____
_____
_____
_____
_____
_____
_____
_____
_____
_____
_____
_____
_____

Day 5

Confidence

Back before the natural hair movement had become a billion-dollar industry, I decided to do the big chop; it was one of the more nerve-wrecking, elected decisions I made as a young adult and yet one of the most profound. There is so much societal emphasis on hair in terms of femininity and beauty. I took chopping off my hair as an act of rebellion to not rely on "pretty "or safe. I also want to prove to people I had the guts to do it (I don't like being underestimated about *ANYTHING*. I had no idea how much cutting my hair would cause me to look at myself, really look at myself for the first time and be happy with who I was and appreciate my features, being bold enough to say "hey I really am beautiful beyond the exterior".

It is amazing how many psychological issues and stereotypes we have that are roped into hair. Cutting off my hair and letting it be free has caused me to question what other things in my life I adhere to because it is what is socially acceptable. The state of being natural for me has become less about hair and so much more about a self-reflective process; learning to look at the person in the mirror and truly love the reflection looking back at me without expectations.

Self-Check:

What is the most natural part of you that you cover up or deny in order to comply with societal norms? Maybe it's time for a BIG CHOP!

_____
_____
_____
_____
_____
_____
_____
_____
_____
_____
_____
_____
_____
_____
_____
_____
_____
_____
_____

Day 6

You are Enough

You are intelligent. You are successful. You are resourceful. You are beautiful, loved and supported. Everything you need is already inside of you. You are enough. I know saying and believing these things can be difficult to do at times, but it is true. Poor decisions and misguided teachings have crippled and tricked us into thinking that we are not whole without a mate, children, the perfect family, friends, or career. Do not believe the lie. Although these are wonderful things that can add to our lives, here is a reminder:

You were already whole without them.

It is very easy to lose yourself when you are trying to find your identity through the eyes of someone else, and for a long time that is what I did until I had a reality check with myself. In an effort to regain who I was, and who I wanted to be I began to search for things that could empower me, fuel me, and help me remember who I was and who I was created to be. I wanted to be a woman of strength, courage, love, and liberation. I wanted to be myself. As simple as it sounds one of the tools I used in the quest of self-discovery was that of music.

I love listening to great music. Anytime I felt myself losing my identity there was always a song that spoke to that brokenness in me. Music can push you forward with inspiration or it can keep you stuck in the past reminiscing on the love and life you once had. The lyrics in a song can be influential, playing on your hopes and dreams as if the words were written specifically with you in mind. So there it was, lyrics from one of my favorite songs:

>"I just wanna be so happy, but the answer lies in me."
>– Mary J. Blige

It is so easy for us to believe we need the support and applause of others in order for us to live out our dreams; this is a lie that many of us have believed for a long time. I want to be happy but is it really possible for things to work in my favor? Could I really become that successful person and do so on my own terms? Can I really live a life I love? The answer to all these questions is YES! I used to believe that I could not be the best version of myself unless someone cosigned for me. I would question my decisions or quickly change my mind when someone did not agree with me; this only crippled my independence. I became dependent on other people to guide my life and found myself going after passions that were not my own. I had to realize that I am my own person and can make decisions for myself: no one else has to agree or understand. I am the change agent. I set the tone and the direction for my life – God and myself of course. People pleasing will burn you out and honestly it is never the other person's fault. We give too much power to those who have no power. Lack of self-esteem, confidence, or fear will keep you stuck but here is the good news:

You don't have to stay stuck.

Begin to trust yourself. Trust that you are intelligent and capable of taking your own life to the next level because that is what you choose to do. Spend time with yourself; there is something great that God has gifted each of us with and that is the will to thrive and be better than the day before. Do not quit on your hopes and dreams just because someone is not on board. You have the power to make it happen.

Self-Check:

Encourage yourself and say: "I can and I will!"

Day 7

The Present is a Gift

For the first year of my daughter's life I was unemployed. I was laid off while on maternity leave and as you could imagine I was totally stressed out. I had always had a job and took care of myself. How was I going to provide for our family now? I felt useless and unfit. With baby in tow I would spend our days at jobs fairs, employment offices, online, you name it, and still no job. Depression started to settle in and I had no energy or desire to spend time with my own daughter. I had a one-track mind and that was to provide as a mother, failing to understand that nurturing was part of the job too. I was losing myself and precious moments with my little one. I was tired all the time and I just wanted to lock myself in the room alone.

I remember having a conversation with my best friend. She reminded me that a lot of women wish they could stay home with their children but were not able to and that was the moment I realized I was complaining and not celebrating. After three miscarriages, I prayed for this little girl and more than anything I wanted to be a great mother. Here she was, beautiful, healthy and I was worried about a job and not my God given gift. Letting go of my worries, I willed my plans to the Lord and seized the amazing opportunity to live in the present. I was on the vacation of my life and I did not have to accumulate work hours to get it. Each day my princess grew and was always showing me something new she had learned; we shared precious moments that I will cherish forever. To top it off her first word was "Mommy!!" and of course this made my husband jealous, but wow. Once she turned one year old, I received a call for a job and I was able to go back to work. My year with her was amazing and it was hard to leave her.

Everyone is so busy planning for their future, but no one understands the joy of living in the present. Stop rushing your life away. The word present is referred to as a gift because that is what it is. Tomorrow is not promised. Take time to live each day and celebrate it. Make every day count. Breathe in the freshness of the air. Feel the wind as it brushes past your cheeks. Enjoy laughs and fun with family and friends. You do not have to neglect your present while planning for your future. These are moments that we will never get back.

Self-check:

Repeat this prayer: Lord help me to see the beauty in each day. Help me to take a moment to rest in your mercy and in your grace. You have my life all planned out. There is nothing that I need that you will not provide. Help me to trust you. Help me to enjoy where I am today because I know you are taking care of my tomorrow. In Jesus Name, Amen.

Day 8

Don't Compare...Conquer!

I remember many times in my adult life when I would allow social media to be my frame of reference for what I deemed as success. I would scroll and it appeared as if everyone was taking fancy trips, making expensive purchases, looked like a great bill of health, and overall "living their best life", meanwhile I was barely making ends meet, did not own a passport and was feeling like I was on a train heading nowhere fast. Not only had I made many false comparisons based on the images people wanted to be seen, but I had begun to fuel jealousy. This poison poured into personal relationships as I held on to feelings of resentment based on perception.

Jealously is a dangerous emotion that can lead to self-destruction. It directly turns your focus away from God and replaces God's sovereignty for your selfishness. You begin to relish in how inept you are and how unfair life or your circumstances are. In those moments you give yourself permission to be the expert, pushing aside and ignoring the plans God may have in store for you. When you size up the gains or accomplishments you see others experiencing, you assume you understand their plight, struggles and testimony; you minimize and remove the great things God has done for them and the great things He certainly can do for you. The feelings of jealousy often lead to depression, self-doubt, binge-eating, and unfortunately self-medicating.

You ultimately control the feelings you allow to manifest on your spirit. The same way you can allow jealousy to take residence in your spirit is the same way you can usher in joy of what you have in front of you. You can begin to get that joy back when you change the scope of your focus to what is important, what matters, and the impact you make in your assignment. If where you are is not good enough, comparing yourself to someone else and becoming envious will not change your circumstances, you have to begin to position yourself to push for more, demand for better and then act on the things that you want.

Self- Check:

You are not entitled to someone else's success.

Day 9

Don't Get Ready - Stay Ready!

There are certain times of the year that I, like so many other people get excited for a change; you know what I am talking about, "New Year...New You." We typically use these markers on the calendar to justify a jump start to new goals, spring cleaning, or resting. But what if we learned to move in whatever season we are in and leverage it to prepare for the season to come?

During times of dormancy, such as autumn and winter, instead of becoming complacent, what if that time was used to consider that all things in nature must go through cycles? Fall and winter mean shorter days and less sun light with noticeable changes in natures scenery; this transition can cause some to become downright depressed. However, just as nature needs a time to rest and remove elements that it no longer needs to survive, we also have seasons in life when we need to remove things that no longer serve our survival purposes and will impede on our growth. Metaphorically speaking, there are times for rebirth, to spring forward, to plant and harvest. Life tends to follow that same rhythm we just choose to not get in sync with it. How much easier would things be if we truly learned to get be still and find the rhythm of our season?

Whatever season you are in, consider it a great moment to self- reflect on your goals, dreams, and aspirations. I want to encourage you to take some to rediscover those aspects of your life that you have ignored, perhaps allowed to go dormant, or have not sprung into manifestation.

Self-Check:

A passive posture never creates change.

Day 10

The Time Has Come

It is amazing what being responsible for someone can do for you. I decided after birthing my daughter the time had come for me to start living on my terms. As she gets older, she has given me gray hair and tried to send me into depression but raising her has been the best wakeup call and the best time of my life. I have become a teacher, a mentor, secret service agent, detective, cheerleader, and an entrepreneur - I have become it all as a Mother.

I never wanted to own a business of my own. I never thought that my ideas were good enough for others to support, even though I really had some pretty amazing visions. However, the work that needed to be put in terrified me. The negative thoughts set in. I cannot be a business owner - I did not finish college! I do not know any business owners! Who would support me? Isn't it crazy how we can have great minds, but be little thinkers? As children we are fearless. We run around touching hot stoves and jumping on and off beds. We had the courage of a lion walking about the jungle full of life and not a care in the world. We grew up and the big world began to consume us, taking over our thoughts formulating false truths. We fall into the traps of needing the approval and praises of others, because in our minds, without it we are unsuccessful. What happened to the lessons once taught by our parents that we can be and do anything we put our minds to?

> "Can I really make it or will I fail?"

What we believe about ourselves will show! If you believe that you can make it, you will NOT fail. In my past years I had allowed negativity and fear to keep me stagnated from living a full and prosperous life. I set major traps of self-doubt, believing that I was not good enough to really have the life of my dreams and God's best for me. Have you ever felt like me? Have you ever sat and thought about how much further you would be in life had you just pushed through some hard times? As we fast forward to where I am now: I have several successful businesses and my daughter is well taken care of; If can do that, surely you can too.

Self-Check:

How are you going to live out the rest of your life? What steps have you put in place that are propelling you to reach your goals? Know that you are a hidden treasure and the time has come for you to live your best life. It is obtainable and you are worthy of it.

_____
_____
_____
_____
_____
_____
_____
_____
_____
_____
_____
_____
_____
_____
_____
_____
_____

Day 11

Commit to the Process

I had the pleasure of attending an empowerment brunch. Prior to my arrival I battled with whether I should even attend at all; I did not really know anyone, networking was not my thing and I did not know what to expect but I had already spent the money to attend. After an hour of going back and forth in my mind I decided to get dressed and go. Meeting new people can be exciting, but for me it was challenging - one challenge had been getting out of the comfort zone of being an introvert and another was conquering fear of the unknown. I wanted to have fun and connect with new people. I wanted to get out my comfort zone and I was up for the challenge. I knew this brunch would aid my venture to connect with like minds and fuel my spirit for the next steps as a business owner.

I arrived at the brunch and was greeted with open arms. Conversing was made easy. We started off with introductions and ice breakers and we even complimented each other. It felt good to receive and give another woman praise for being fabulous; I began to feel comfortable in a room full of amazing entrepreneurs and I was not the least intimidated. "What was I so afraid of before?", I thought. Then it was time for Q & A and each woman was asked to answer a question. I could not hide. I chose not to excuse myself from the table, but, instead, began to shrink. Small talk is one thing but sharing detailed pieces about your vision and your business is another. These women were well versed in their field and I was just starting out. "When was the last time you were adventurous?", the hostess asked. With my knees shaking and my heart beating fast, I mustered up the courage and told my story of how I ended up in the room. The women looked at me with amazement and surprise; they could not believe that I was nervous and anxious to attend. One of the women stated she thought I was part of the speaking panel. She went on to say when I walked in the room she felt a change in the atmosphere; she saw confidence, strength, wisdom, and wealth inside of me. She said I lit up the room. I felt relieved once more and thought, wow all I did was be myself. I shared the information I knew from my heart and that was enough.

I am saying all this to say: how we view ourselves is important. If you see yourself as insignificant you will operate out of that lie. Traveling into a new dimension of self-assurance and boldness is not an easy task when you are taking a leap of faith. Whether it be a business venture or just getting out to meet new people there may certain anxieties that you will face - you are not alone in that. The bible says:

"be anxious for nothing, but in everything by prayer and supplication, with thanksgiving, let your requests be made known to God; and the peace of God, which surpasses all understanding, will guard your hearts and minds through Christ Jesus."

- Phil 4:6-7

After I let my hair down, relaxed and took time to breathe I began to enjoy myself even more. As a business woman, I committed to the process of becoming a better me. I committed to the process of teaching and sharing what

I do professionally to help our communities. I committed to the process of teaming up with other powerful women with the same goals and drive as me. I committed to step in a world of the unknown to make sure it changes for the better. You have limitless possibilities to grow as a person, make life changing impact, meet other bosses and be supported and loved by those who understand your process and what it takes to break barriers. Had I stayed home feeling defeated, unworthy, undervalued and questioning myself, I would have never been in the room making lifelong connections. We have to learn to leave the place of familiar and the feelings of fear. These two things will have you missing out on what can change the lives of others and have you miss out on becoming a better you.

Being committed is a process that many fail at but that does not have to be you. There is something in life that you desire. You have the power to get it. Committing to the process in faith and in deed allows you to receive all that God has purposed for you. How bad do you want it? It will take discipline, trust in your Creator and committing no matter what the uncertainties are. There will be highs and lows but your highs will overshadow the lows when you show up. Decide what you want to do and be willing to do it. It will be worth it in the end.

Self-Check:

What processes do you need to commit to in order to have the life you desire?

_____
_____
_____
_____
_____
_____
_____
_____
_____
_____
_____
_____
_____
_____
_____
_____
_____
_____
_____
_____
_____

Day 12

Pint-Size Wisdom: "Dare to be Different"

As a parent, you learn to not only to be a teacher but student, as children seem to be born with a certain amount of wisdom and intuitiveness.

One morning my three year-old woke up in a particularly happy mood and after getting his usual shot of milk, went to the refrigerator and grabbed a pack of hot dogs. He came to me quite sincerely and request to have one for breakfast, to which I replied "hotdogs and what?" He looked at me and said, "mustard". His father heard his request for hot dogs and I could tell from his silence, that this was a breakfast selection he was not extremely pleased about, however I was not particularly opposed to the option, but instead, just thought it was weird.

We decided to give in and allow him to have a "breakfast of champions" provided he eat a fruit as a side item. The more I thought of his unusual request the more my brain began to rationalize it. Was the idea of a hot dog in the morning that odd? If I were to flatten that meat byproduct out and call it sausage, it would be completely acceptable right? Right. It was not the meat I had a problem with it was the packaging.

How often am I or we (for that matter) apprehensive to look at things differently or go outside of the box. Often there is fear or trepidation, even feelings of being misunderstood or judged for going against the grain, only to realize that being different can often open up a world of new possibilities. I was challenged by my son to look at his breakfast meat option as more than just an option for the Ballpark or a last resort when mommy does not want to cook. Because I had assigned a "role" and "rule" for hotdogs I almost not only caused a morning tantrum and stifled his culinary creativity but I would have missed the opportunity to investigate other areas of my life that I may be unwilling to reinvent and see from another angle all because I have created the comfortable rule of where it fits in my life. Who knew there could be a life lesson from a hotdog?

Self-Check:

Learn to constantly question, reinvent, and create a world outside of the box. You will be amazed how much it will change your perspective.

Day 13

An Outward Look to Reflect an Inside Change

My hair was honey blonde, fiery, and I was ready to take on the world or so I thought. Smiling on the outside, but broken, bruised, and very confused on the inside, I felt like a prisoner held captive to the life I was so desperately trying to forget. It was getting harder to make the "right" decisions that would grow my business and keep my family happy. I could not believe it! I had worked so hard on my exterior, creating and aligning what I thought was going to drive an internal reset process. What was the problem? I thought if I looked good I would feel good – but I did not. We are so good at dressing up the outside; from the makeup, hair and down to the outfit, we sure do know how to put it all together. If we are going to thrive at life and dare to be all we are created to become, we must recognize there are changes that will need to happen on the inside. We have to be so focused on the end that everything that we do are steps toward that goal.

When was the last time you felt happy, fulfilled, and satisfied with yourself and the way that things are going? These are questions that you should ask yourself. No matter how much we go to the salon or take shopping sprees, no amount of dressing up will rid the junk we have filling up on the inside of us especially if we have suffered for years. We must empty out the mess so that the message can shine through, impact our lives and the lives of others for the better.

Here is the good news: you have not seen your best days yet! We all must start somewhere. Allow the newness in your life to become the driving force. Looking good on the outside will not fix any internal issues, but hey it is a start, just make a conscious decision not to stop there.

Self-Check:

When you look good you should feel good and vice versa. Are you feeling good and looking good? If these are not matching up it is time to take a deeper look on the inside of yourself.

_____
_____
_____
_____
_____
_____
_____
_____
_____
_____
_____
_____
_____
_____
_____
_____
_____
_____
_____
_____
_____
_____
_____

Day 14

It's Okay

"It's okay" seems to be a very simple statement of agreement until it is applied to a situation or problem beyond our control. When life throws unexpected curve balls, "it's okay" is no longer simple and most certainly not satisfying. In life, the unexpected is sure to happen causing detours or adjustments to be made to our regularly scheduled programs. When this happens, you will have to ask yourself this question:

Do I panic and lose my cool or do I take a moment and say you know what "It's okay."

I remember getting ready for our first family portrait. Everyone was so excited except my newborn who was extremely fussy on this day. There we were, next in line and then it happened! The baby princess had thrown up all over her matching Sunday's best and I was horrified! In that moment I had to make a decision: be upset or make an adjustment. My husband looked at me, and before he could get a word out I said
"It's okay, I prepared for this!" Like superwoman I quickly changed the baby's clothes and we were able to take our picture and my joy was not interrupted.

Can you think of a time you just quit when life became challenging? How many dreams are we willing to leave on pillows before we say "no matter what happens it's okay, I will accomplish this?"

We cannot control the unexpected but deciding to take the positive route allows for no interruptions of our peace and joy; we are then able to keep control of our feelings, making necessary adjustments to accomplish the goals we set for ourselves. Saying "it's okay" does not have to be a passive aggressive statement. It can also be a statement of power that breathes life in a world that says our hopes and dreams are powerless. Saying "it's okay" can be the key that opens the door and makes known that no matter what adjustments are needed, we will stay focus on the goal not the problem or distraction. It's deciding to stop at nothing to ensure that our dreams come off the pillow and become realities in our lives.

Self-Check:

Although we cannot control the unexpected, we can prepare for it.

Day 15

Be Disruptive

Sitting silent and cute can only get you so far in life. To activate change it requires action, motivation, which by definition is "goal directed and disruptive". Now when I say be disruptive, I certainly am not suggesting physical destruction, but I am talking about being so uncomfortable with where you are that it demands something to change not just internally but it must also manifest in your environment. Disruption forces a change in the norm, the typical and the mundane and serves as a break from the continuation of some activity. I have found that this change only occurs when I have become sick and tired of being sick and tired. When circumstances out of my control change a pattern of events which means that while some things will always be out of our control, we hold a lot of power in creating the change we wish to see. Getting unstuck, to me, is the hardest part of the entire process but it is in those moments I have had to really reach for God and ask Him to remove my complacency, to stir up a spirit of disruption for me and when He honors that request I have to be ready to move.

"Lazy people want much but get little but those who work hard will prosper." (Proverbs 13:4)

Now truth is, even when God presses upon you and begins to move you, you will not always want to do it and no you will not always be in the mood, but when you are focused on a goal that goal does not require your moods it requires your consistency. Learn to be comfortable in discomfort and do not settle even when you think the work is done. Take pride in your accomplishments knowing that within you God's gifts can go so much farther, so find people who will encourage you and then unapologetically become disruptive.

Self-Check:

When you think about your goals and dreams, what areas of your life need to be disrupted and destroyed in order to begin to change and create?

_____
_____
_____
_____
_____
_____
_____
_____
_____
_____
_____
_____
_____
_____
_____
_____
_____
_____

Day 16

Don't Drop the Glass Balls

As women most of us can relate to feeling as though we are the owner and operator of an internal circus with our main stage act of being a juggler. I remember talking with an older lady who, while I began to explain to her all of my obligations and all of the legitimate reasons I had not connected with her, politely dismissed everything I said and replied to me "we all juggle balls, but it is important not to drop the glass ones."
Not only was I beyond irritated with this statement I was also puzzled because at that moment all of these *balls* seemed to be glass.

I was not only stretched in every direction imaginable, but I was also beyond worn out. I would love to say that I did not have a full meltdown but took the time needed to rest and reassess but that is not true *(I in fact had a full melt down)*. I allowed myself to come to near burnout which caused me to sit with myself and figure out what I was juggling and to question was it all necessary. In life there are glass balls also known as "matters of priority" and then there are things we falsely allow to take precedence in our lives; these are generally the things that steal our happiness, and cause mental, physical, and emotional fatigue. While balance is an elusive phenomenon as nothing is ever quite 50/50, you can decide what has your attention and what needs your attention. Place your focus on the things that matter, which may cause you to choose and spend your time more wisely. We all get the same amount of time each day but where you direct your energy is a matter of choice. You are precious, so are your gifts, so is your time.

Self-Check:

Glass may break but YOU will not; shift your energy to what matters most.

Day 17

Setting Boundaries (Part 1)

We often think of the need to set boundaries for others in an effort to safeguard our well-being, but how often do we set boundaries and limits on ourselves? Are you aware of what your threshold is, or what it should be? Do you command charge over what you allow to invade you space, your time, and your spirit or do you accept whatever comes your way and then sulk in the unhappiness it brings? Just as important as it is to utilize the word "no" to express what you are capable of and what you can produce, it is equally important to be in charge of your boundaries. I find that people who are often easily overwhelmed, anxious, irritable, exhausted, or down are those whose have not created limits in their lives. Everything that comes to you is not in your best interest and does not deserve your time and attention. Learn to decipher things that are purposeful and make sense for the path you are on. If it does not fit into your goals then it is unnecessary and should be removed. Even the best of us who seem to have it "all together" (whatever that actually means) will inevitably allow foolishness, behaviors, jobs, relationships to ensue much longer than they should, but once you recognize it, the choice becomes yours as to what steps need to occur next.

Self-Check:

No one wants an invitation to your pity party. Set the boundaries you need and create the space mentally, emotionally, and environmentally that you desire on your terms and on your time.

_____
_____
_____
_____
_____
_____
_____
_____
_____
_____
_____
_____
_____
_____
_____
_____
_____
_____
_____
_____

Day 18

Set the Boundaries Then Clean Your Clutter (Part 2)

I am a huge "journal-er" – I always have been and always will be. While in preparation for this book, I found a note I wrote to myself February 2, 2016 which read:

"You can allow fear to speak louder than God, and then wonder why you cannot hear Him."

Sometimes even louder than fear is the sound of mental clutter which can be loud, distracting and defeating. Proverbs 18:6 says:

"a man's [woman] gift maketh room for him and bringeth him before great men."

My question is, have you cleaned your own space to receive the gift God has given you? We can clutter our space with so much noise and distraction that there is no room for anything else leaving your clutter guilty of suffocating your gift – the purpose and destiny of your life. At the same token if you look at the Common English Bible version of the same text it states:

"A gift opens the way for access to important people."

Who could God connect and give you access to, or even better, who could God send to access you, your gifts and your talents if you allow space to receive it? Discover what crowds your space mentally and environmentally and organize it, clean it up, or remove it. Learn to keep only the things that serve your higher purpose, and then, not only will you be able to hear God more clearly but there will be space for Him to take charge.

Self-Check:

It's time to do some internal inventory.

Day 19

God Did Not Give Them the Vision, So Do Not Expect Them to Understand Your Dreams.

My son recently came to me upset because he got tired of telling his classmates that what they think of him or his ideas is merely their opinion. I tried to affirm him by reminding him how extremely amazing he is, and how these kids probably were not worth really investing time or energy in, especially as they seem to not share similar interest; at the end of this conversation I looked him straight in the eye and said, "Listen you aren't for everybody and everybody isn't for you, and that is okay."

For years I have given myself the self-description of being "an acquired taste" - you either like me or you do not. This has served me well in taking the pressure and responsibility of how someone views me off my list of things to cognitively attend to. Whatever their thoughts or feelings, I cannot allow that to derail or distract me from being fully accepting of who I am or being willing to share all the great in me with the world. The amount of time and energy expended toward people who are not invested in you will reap no return or benefit. It is so important to authentically encourage others and to be reminded that we do not need the approval of others but that we should strive to attain worth from a higher source.

Decide that their approval does not matter, it does not qualify you and it will not propel you toward your goals. You do not need permission to pursue your passion you just have to be present. Learn to encourage yourself.

I believe I was born with an entrepreneurial spirit with dreams of having my own business, and one day I got up the nerve to share my ideas with someone very close to me; every idea I gave seemed to be shot down and finally my loved one asked the most gut-wrenching question:

"Would anybody really pay for that?"

While the question was valid, I would really have no way of knowing this unless I pursued it; even with the best risk analysis you have to be willing to invest in your dreams. I allowed that one opinion to cripple my dreams for YEARS leaving me afraid to share any of myself with the world and willing to succumb to a typical and safe 9 to 5 job. What I had not yet realized was that it is okay for others to question your dreams, and even think what you are pursing is beyond your understanding, but you have to be secure in the gifts you have and what your dream is. People can only give you information based on their experiences which are unique to them, remember that. Your dream was meant for you and only you can interpret the way you wish for it to manifest into reality.

Self-Check:

Just because they don't get "it" doesn't mean you should not pursue it.

Day 20

Create the Community You Deserve

I am a bona-fide girl's girl and my passion for human services lends me to readily be available to attend to others needs, but I am learning especially as I continue to explore and discover who I am, that I need the comfort of authentic relationships. I find that it is so important as we journey through life that we do not do it alone. All of us were not born into safe, loving homes and many were often hurt by those closest to us. These circumstances can leave us so hurt, and so full of mistrust that we isolate ourselves from true companionship and sisterhood when it is an innate yearning. For me, although I do not open up or share myself readily with others due to preconceive notions, feelings of inadequacy, rejection, and past pains, as I have gotten older I have come to acknowledge how truly invaluable the blessing of friendship is.

Having a strong and intentional circle of people who not only support you but hold you accountable is important. I find, for me, it is in those safe places that I can vulnerably share my ideas and this same place serves as a place where I feel the most safe and protected. The right bench of people, who may not all be female and may not look anything like you, will not always agree with you or share your vision and dreams but they will see you, recognize your worth and get you who you are. It is so rare that these types of environments or circle of friendships organically come to fruition, I have found that it is always God led, and therefore purposeful.

Honor this gift from God by showing up, being present with who you are and where you are mentally and emotionally at that moment. With your circle, take a chance and be honest and give mutual respect. Take the time to discover the depth of the relationships that God orchestrated and extend what you have to offer to your friends by being available; learn to leverage their gifts in talents so that you can build each other up. Make a decision to allow others to support you and see you at your worse, knowing that you will find that in those moments, you are still so worthy of love. Lastly, be open enough, even if you cannot open your heart, to start with at least opening your mind and your arms in a posture to receive all the goodness a strong community can provide.

Self-Check:

Your time is precious choose to share it with those that matter and who know that You matter.

Day 21

You are the Superpower

Four women from different cultures and backgrounds decided to come together for a goal to impact change in national legislation. History was made as men and children joined in support of over 500,000 women standing together for their rights and the rights of others during the 2017 Women's March in Washington, D.C.; it was reported that around 673 marches took place worldwide on all continents to join in the efforts. This movement like many others changed my life forever.

There is something to be said about a confident person who stands out in a crowd. Women have grown far from just being visible and not heard. In addition to taking care of our homes we have become business owners and influential leaders in our communities. There is no harm is being called eye candy because we make life look yummy, but we are so much more than just a pretty face. Sisterhoods have been formed with missions to equally live meaningful lives and secure the future for our families for decades. We consistently suspend the myth that women are jealous and cannot get along; "Reality TV" is not the reality of most.

As much as we can stand together, it takes the decision of an individual to be part of the solution and not the problem. Are you willing to disturb your normalcy in order to see the desires of your heart manifest into reality? Too often we have great master plans, but they lay stagnate in journals and tucked away in forgetful places collecting dust. We have left our purpose and vision in the hands of others that cannot see us beyond our current state. What If I told you that you are already successful and everything you do brings forth a harvest? How would you look at your life? Would you then operate out of lack or abundance? One of the most disturbing things to see is a person with potential wasting time and energy on things that they do not enjoy because they do not believe in themselves. That will not be the case for you.

There are 24 hours in a day. When your feet hit the floor that is when your time starts. What you do with that time matters. Meet the challenges of every goal. Make a plan to get things done. If you have a vision write it down and make it plain. If you have already written the vision dust the ideas off and start making things happen.

Self-Check:
You are the superpower.

Day 22

Reset! Recharge! Relax

I am such a firm believer that God called for the Sabbath not because He needed to rest during creation but because He knew that unless it was a commandment, we would likely not do it - common sense would not kick in and remind us to rest. We live in a culture where it is expected that your entire day is full of work, meetings, and other's expectations. To take time away to rejuvenate can sometimes be seen as laziness or a "new age" theory but truth is everything in nature is called to rest. I learned the term "active rest" during one of my many attempts to get in shape. The body does not maximize muscle gains by constantly exerting the same muscles each day: you have to work out other areas and allow the muscles a time for recovery. During this time, you remove stress from that area while continuing to do lighter activities. Active recovery actually gives better and faster results than constant weight - lifting.

My apologies if that analogy completely missed you because working out is not your "thing." Let's try farming, as most of us enjoy the comforts of food. In order to produce a good harvest, soil must rest - this is called field fallow or crop rotation. Failure to do so can result in yielding less produce, less fertile soil as its nutrients are not being replenished and can be more vulnerable to erosion. Still nothing? Let's skip the other great analogies I have so that I can offer a few simple suggestions when you are feeling burnt out from the grind and yet the thought of taking a break is out of your comfort zone.

- Practice self- care (if this concept is foreign to you it should make it's way to the very top of your list.

- Make your moves thoughtful and not mindless

- Prioritize what is important

- Do not overtask for the sake of being busy

- Do not be busy - be purposeful

- Chose to always have a reserve left for yourself.

Self-Check:

How do you reset your intentions and energy?

_____
_____
_____
_____
_____
_____
_____
_____
_____
_____
_____
_____
_____
_____
_____
_____
_____
_____
_____
_____
_____
_____

Day 23

Foundation Matters

Have you ever been in a relationship and yet felt like you were next to a stranger? More often than most of us would like to admit, we chose a partner and get into relationships based on external interests. That person looks good, smells nice, and has a job, fulfills an immediate convenience and not a long-term connection. We are too afraid to dig deeper for fear that Mr. Perfect might actually be Mr. Pathetic and we have to start all over again. Sometimes we have not gone deep enough with knowing who we are to even attract who we deserve. When we seek out superficial relationships, we cheat ourselves of precious time and undervalue our worth.

If you begin a relationship based on a façade, accept the reality that it will not last - period. This goes for both parties; you must be okay with revealing who you are. Beyond the lashes and a bright smile, you have to be open to letting that person know that you do not have it *all* together (but you are working on it).

Think of choosing a mate like investing in a property without taking the time to do a proper inspection or appraisal. Once you are invested, even when the foundation is bad, you do not want to walk away. The same goes for a relationship: many times we realize the foundation of our relationships are not of sound structure, but we continue to remodel and add to the look of the structure further damaging the integrity of what we thought was a good "house". The truth is, there was no value in the property or relationship to begin with.

The only true solution is to tear it down completely to the ground; often even as a metaphor this sounds horrible and like a lot of work but, without tearing down a poor structure, what you built is not going to last. This process can happen more than once if you continue to build and add with the wrong materials. Unless you are willing to take the time to build with materials such as trust, honesty, integrity, and vulnerability, as well as, ensure the foundation is strong, inevitably you will need to cut your losses and walk away!

Self-Check:

Are the foundations in your life solid?

Day 24

Perception is Reality

Sometimes moments may look like and appear to be a missed opportunity, doors closed in your face, and rejection. Often, we are not fueled to make a change until changing is the only option left. There may be times when you feel completely alone; but question how many people do you need to be successful? The answer is just one, and that is YOU. How many people need to believe in your dreams? You only need one. You hold the key to every open door, but you also must position yourself to move toward the opportunities that are aligned with your focus and your passion. We allow ourselves to get so full of doubt that we talk ourselves out of even attempting to try. We ask the questions "why":

Why didn't I get promoted?

Why didn't I go back to school?

"Why am I not married?"

Instead of asking "why not", ask for that promotion or go back to school. Regarding relationships, deal with your issues so that you will be ready to receive a God given companionship if He wills it. I am a firm believer that we continue to feel rejection until we are ready to receive, not just with the words we say, but with our actions, with our intentions, and with our energy. Remember, we are the change agents of our lives. Start today and focus on the "why not": this has always pushed me to challenge and remind myself that while I may never feel as though I am great, there is greatness within me. After giving birth to my first child the saddest thought was not having enough time with him and someone else raising him because I had to go to work. I was blessed to be able to stay home with him for several months before getting a new job and truth be told he was well loved and cared for while I was away, shortly after that I was laid off but happy to stay home with my toddler. Fast forward several years when my second child entered the world and my management job was inflexible with my new life change - I made the decision to not only continue to pursue school (on loans) but to leave that job; for the next 5 years I struggled to get hired, had a third child and was living pay check to pay check. I often found myself lamenting to God that I wanted better because I had experience and degrees, yet no one was hiring me. Through this I never stopped talking to God but often found myself frustrated with Him. Then one day the Lord brought me to

Philippians 4: 11-13

"I am not saying this because I am in need, for I have learned to be content whatever the circumstances. I know what it is to be in need, and I know what it is to have plenty. I have learned the secret of being content in any and every situation, whether well fed or hungry, whether living in plenty or in want. I can do all this through him who gives me strength."

God was showing me that I am great in Him and not in what I have. I had prayed to have the time and ability to stay home with my babies to raise them and yet when He made that a reality I whined from a lack of resources; all the while neither my family nor I never lacked in our needs being met. In that season, God humbled my spirit, made me rely completely on Him, His timing, and His sovereignty and taught me to find gratitude with where I was.

I began to cherish the moments longer while using that time to focus on my next steps, establishing my LLC, and even making it to the Stellar Awards. My circumstances did not change until my mindset and focus did.

Self-Check:

Change your perception to align with you purpose.

Day 25

Access Granted

"Close your eyes and center yourself. Take a deep breath in through your nose 1.2.3….and exhale through your mouth 1.2.3…. Slowly relax your shoulders and let your mind rest. We are going to do this once more, just allow your body to relax. Forget about the troubles of the day and be in this moment." I had listened to this meditation audio for weeks and I was still as tense as before I started only now, more anxious and unrelaxed. This was not working. Calm down is what my friend kept saying to me – "you have to calm down this is a good thing." I was preparing for one of the biggest moments of my life and I was literally having a panic attack. I could not breathe; I had been holding my breath most of the day off and on. My hands were shaking so much I could not even put in my contacts. It was time to announce the top nominee's for Internet Radio Station of the Year. Our station's name was called the screams and the applause that filled the room will forever be beautiful sounds in my ears. All my anxiety went away. How did I get here? What had I done right to be amongst legends and so much talent? I do not know but I was here and I was grateful.

I had tried so many times to talk myself out of my blessings because I did not believe that I was worthy of answered prayers - to be successful on my terms, for God to take me to higher levels in my education and in my knowledge of my craft or that my gift would actually make room for me and put me before great men. I did not believe, but God kept saying "Your access has been granted." We have been conditioned so much to accept disappointment that we have no clue what answered prayer looks like. Even in our disbelief there is a big part of us that says there is something great ahead if we keep moving forward. Whether the push is our faith or just plain curiosity, forward is a great direction to take.

What I have come to discover is that we must start believing in ourselves. We have the keys to every door God would allow us to go through because He wants us to succeed. Remember He wants us to prosper in every area of our lives. Jeremiah 29:11 reminds us:

"For I know the plans that I have for you says the Lord, plans to prosper you and not harm you, plans to give you hope, and a future. If it weren't true, the Lord would not have said it."

You may not believe in the God I serve, but I am adding my faith to your faith that you will receive whatsoever your heart desires and that you will start believing that your access has been granted.

Self-Check:

Now that you know you have the keys, what doors will you begin to open?

Day 26

Do the Work

God is very capable of putting people and things in our lives that will make business, home life and even ourselves very comfortable, but sometimes, we'll have to get our hands dirty. Play time is over and now it is time to put in the work. We have been students of our own lives. It is necessary that we put action to what we have learned over the years. Application is necessary to carry out our desires, purpose, and vision.

As a child I grew up loving to read, but I struggled to remember what I read. If someone read to me, I could tell them exactly what they said but when I read the same story, it would have to be read several times to comprehend. This became such a struggle that I vowed that I would not read again – frustration screamed loudly, "Audio please!" But because I am a go getter I innately never allow myself to be crippled by temporary setbacks. I began to take every FREE reading comprehension and writing class I could. There were sleepless nights and I declined hanging out with friends just to learn all I could - I even took speech classes. This meant that I was all work and no play. My romantic life was non-existent, and I was okay with that. I used the tips learned in my classes and progressed in my comprehension. One of the things I found was that I had to slow down and pay attention. I was rushing through the reading instead of studying the words and how they formed the actual story. My mind would always be on more than one thing, so I had to learn how to focus.

Here we are today- I am writing and you are reading. My purpose and vision is to share my truths so that you will not feel alone in the challenges you may face. You can overcome them. My challenges and my work turned in to countless victories and so will yours. Trust me, you got this - I am rooting for you.

You are working a purpose and a vision. There may be late nights and early mornings. Like me your social and romantic life may have to take the back seat, but I promise you that if you keep doing the work it will pay off.

Self-Check:

"Success is no accident. It is hard work, perseverance, learning, studying, sacrifice, and most of all, love of what you are doing."

-Unknown

Day 27

Go On and Be Great: The Movement

I created this movement to support and celebrate unsung heroes - those who have been overlooked and caught in the crossfire between living life at the top and hitting rock bottom. This movement was created for those who have made dealing with the issues of life seem like a piece of cake.

My grandmother had worked her whole life. She started taking care of others at the age of 13 and had to quit school in the sixth grade. I watched her raise nine children, a host of grandchildren and great grandchildren along with serving as the mother of the community, a pastor, sister, and friend. I never heard her complain and she was often overlooked and did not receive all the appreciation that was certainly due to her. For as long as I can remember every morning, she would get up around 6 a.m. and sing her favorite song:

"Lord I just want to thank You."

She never asked for anything in return. Just waking up was enough for her to be happy. Much like most of us, Granny was so used to keeping things afloat she neglected taking care of herself or celebrating her accomplishments. There are so many beautiful memories of our time together such as our weekly rides where we took food to the sick, rode her friends back and forth to the market or the dollar store to get things for their DIY projects, and my favorite, thrifting! My Granny never wanted to miss a day of church; if the doors were open, she expected to be there. When my grandmother died, I did not think I was going to recover. My heart was broken in a way that left me in a million pieces, but I knew I had to go on. I had shared my hopes and dreams with my Grandmother, and she was supposed to stay alive to see all of them manifested. I was stuck and in that place nothing mattered. All my plans and all the blueprints of my future were at a standstill. I could not move from that place. I thought "What is it all for, if I am just going to lose everything I have worked so hard for which is and has always been my family?" Though I was dealing with grief I still managed to get up every day, continue my daily routine and smiled like I had not a care in the world.

Some would say I was suppressing my feelings acting unbothered. I say I was walking in the scripture that says "God's grace is sufficient" to hold me up high even when I am going through valleys. Time does not stop - it keeps ticking and you will have to do the same. Every day is not a bad day; know that there are good days too and whichever you zone in on sets the tone for your life. Please understand that just because others see the glass half empty, it does not mean you have to. You can choose to have joy, show love, and enjoy peace even in the midst of a storm. It is your choice. Choose wisely. Go on and be great - you do not need permission to be something you already are. Greatness does not stop when you have more month than money and it does not stop because there is a hiccup in your plans. By the way, it certainly does not stop because your relationship ended or that business deal did not pan out. Greatness is a part of you – it is in your blood, bones and DNA. You can suppress it, but it will always show up as a reminder that you cannot stay down. You must get up. Nothing can stop the greatness inside of you and nothing can take it away.

Self-Check:

Everything gets better from here.

Day 28

Play to Win

The super bowl is the most viewed and attended event during football season. Stadiums are overflowing with fans from near and far. Homes across the country are filled with fun, laughter and screaming adults as they root for their favorite teams to win. There are two major positions that are played, offense or defense. The primary function of the offense is to score touchdowns through a series of different plays. The defense's primary function is to prevent the offense from scoring by tackling players or causing turnovers (fumbles). No matter what side of the team the players are one only one thing matters - WINNING. Months of training and small victories lead up to the big and final game - nothing before this moment matters. As the team prepares for the game to start, they can hear the crowd going wild in anticipation. I have seen interviews of players whose adrenaline has been so high they cannot keep still. Right before kick-off, the team huddles together for pep talks and encouragement. Everything has led up to this very moment: training, losses, lessons learned, blood, sweat, tears, and I am sure some fears but it is game time.

As with football when your feet hit the ground it should symbolize that you are present and ready not just to play the game, but to WIN. No opposition or set back matters. You trained for this and you have won the battles of fear, self-doubt, frustration, and other things that would come against your greatness countless times already and will continue to do it repeatedly. Sometimes you may have to play offense – being so focused on the goal that having to use different plays does not take you off focus at all. Other times you may have to play defense- blocking naysayers, dream killers, and even negative thoughts. Whatever the position know that you did not just come to play but you came to win!

Self-Check:

You have been chosen to play in the big game called Life. You are not here by chance. You are here intentionally to be the light and inspiration for yourself and others. Every moment, every experience has brought you to this place, this moment, and this time. You have been trained to win and whatever winning looks like to you know that it is achievable. Look in the mirror and say, "I've got the juice!"

_____
_____
_____
_____
_____
_____
_____
_____
_____
_____
_____
_____
_____
_____

Day 29

Celebrate Always

I love a good party but planning a celebration can be nerve wracking. There is so much to decide and execute. What's the theme, how many guests, what food to feed the guests and what kind of music should there be? No matter what preparation needs to take place, a party is not a party if no one shows up to celebrate. It is important to celebrate the accomplishments of yourself and others. Celebrate every blessing even if it does not come in the package you were expecting and be appreciative of what you already have. Countless others wish they could be in your shoes. They wish they could be like you and have what you have. When you encounter such persons be sure to encourage them to stand strong in themselves and be grateful for their own blessings. All blessings from God are tailor made to fit our needs and to fulfill His purpose for us; it is a win-win situation. Do not compare, complain, or compete with others. It takes me to handle my journey and it will take you to handle yours; this is why we must continue to help one another thrive. While you are celebrating others, do not forget to celebrate yourself! You have worked hard to get where you are today, mentally, emotionally, and spiritually. Treat yourself out to dinner or a good time of your choosing because you truly deserve every bit of it. I never understood why doing things for ourselves has been labeled as being selfish. I am a big advocate for self-care and alone time and you should be too! You are no good to anyone if you are not good to yourself.

Self-Check:

When was the last time you took time out for yourself? If you have to, think long and hard, I encourage you to plan that date and have yourself a celebrating good time!

_____
_____
_____
_____
_____
_____
_____
_____
_____
_____
_____
_____
_____
_____
_____
_____
_____
_____
_____
_____
_____

Day 30

Better Than Ever

You are so much greater than what you realize, and the world can benefit from you being a part of it but only you can initiate your journey. Truth is, you can read this book and countless others that push you towards change. Books that make you contemplate what you want out of life, and even inspire you. But there is no quick fix towards greatness. With change comes resistance and obstacles and days when you want to give up and question yourself time and time again. Making the decision to bet on you, your talent, your worth is the most vulnerable and scary thing you will ever do; you ultimately get to decide whether to live the life you want and deserve or settle for what life brings your way.

Many of us are taught that there is no fear in God, and His plans for you extend so much farther and higher than even your greatest dreams can imagine, yet we hesitate to use these God given gifts. Stop following social media and start leading social media. Stop "pinning" inspirational quotes unless they motivate you to action. Do not subscribe to another You Tube channel to watch people tell you what you already know, but instead, subscribe to your higher calling and the idea that greatness is within you.

You have something to give to the world. Greatness may not translate into lots of "likes" (but it could), millions of dollars (but it could), saving lives or creating the next best thing (although it could). Your greatness comes when you began to use the things you are naturally good at to bring joy into your life and others -when what you have to offer goes outside of just you and your comfort zone and begins to bless those around you. Stop wishing, start praying, planning, and planting yourself purposefully to what you deserve. This is the best time of your life to begin because it's where God has you. You are *Better Than Ever* and your better is **now!**

Self-Check:

You have everything you need for the life you deserve, but you have to believe it and then go after it.

Connect With Us!

Email: snlbetterthanever@gmail.com

LaRissa Oxner

Facebook: www.facebook.com/larissa.oxner

Instagram: Ris_Rene

Sherry Smalls

Facebook: www.facebook.com/reinventeddestiny

Twitter: SherryReinvents

Instagram: reinventeddestiny

www.reinventeddestiny.com

Made in the USA
Columbia, SC
14 March 2020